P9-CBR-427

Pan Am Flight 103

Other titles in the *American Disasters* series:

Pan Am Flight 103

Terrorism Over Lockerbie

Karen Bornemann Spies

Enslow Publishers, Inc.

40 Industrial Road   PO Box 38
Box 398   Aldershot
Berkeley Heights, NJ 07922   Hants GU12 6BP
USA   UK
http://www.enslow.com

Library of Congress Cataloging-in-Publication Data

Spies, Karen Bornemann.
   Pan Am flight 103 : terrorism over Lockerbie / Karen Bornemann Spies.
      p. cm. — (American disasters)
   Summary: Provides an account of the bombing of Pan Am Flight 103, which
occurred over Lockerbie, Scotland, in December of 1988.
   Includes bibliographical references (p.   ) and index.
   ISBN 0-7660-1788-5
      1. Pan Am Flight 103 Bombing Incident, 1988—Juvenile literature.
   2. Terrorism—Europe—Juvenile literature. 3. Terrorism—United States—Juvenile
literature. 4. Bombing investigation—Scotland—Lockerbie—Juvenile literature.
   [1. Pan Am Flight 103 Bombing Incident, 1988. 2. Terrorism. 3. Bombing investigation.] I. Title. II. Series.
   HV6431 .S65 2003
   363.12'465'094147—dc21
                                                        2002003889

Printed in the United States of America

10 9 8 7 6 5 4 3 2 1

Illustration Credits: AP/Wide World Photos.

Cover Illustration: AP/Wide World Photos.

Contents

*R*osebank Terrace resident Maxwell Kerr takes a walk near the neighboring town of Lockerbie, Scotland, in December 1998. The quiet village was located on the flight route of Pan Am Flight 103 ten years earlier.

CHAPTER 1

December 21, 1988

It was four days before Christmas in 1988, and London's Heathrow Airport was bustling with activity. The passengers preparing to board Pan American Airways Flight 103 were filled with holiday spirit. Among them were military personnel and business people who looked forward to spending time at home with their families. Thirty-five passengers were students from Syracuse University in New York who were returning home after spending a semester studying in London.

Some of those boarding were originally scheduled to be on earlier flights. Thomas Ammerman, a shipping company executive, missed his noon flight because he had to attend a business meeting. Three-year-old Suruchi Rattan and her family missed an earlier flight when her two-year-old brother, Anmol, became ill.

In all, 243 passengers and sixteen crew members would board Pan Am 103. The three members of the flight crew were Captain James B. MacQuarrie, age fifty-five;

First Officer Ray R. Wagner, age fifty-two; and Flight Engineer Jerry D. Avritt, age forty-six. The flight attendants came from several different countries, including Great Britain, France, Sweden, West Germany, Spain, and the United States. Twenty-year-old Stacie Franklin was working on her first flight for Pan Am.

Pan Am 103 was scheduled to fly from London to New York's John F. Kennedy Airport (known as JFK). A connecting flight, Pan Am 103A, originated in Frankfurt, in what was then West Germany. When Pan Am 103A arrived at Heathrow, passengers and luggage continuing on to the United States were transferred from the Boeing 727 to a larger 747 jumbo jet for Pan Am 103's flight over the Atlantic Ocean. Many new passengers also boarded the plane in London.

The 747 scheduled for the flight, named *Maid of the Seas*, was supposed to depart from Heathrow at 6:00 P.M. The flight was delayed, however, because the plane from Frankfurt was late. Finally, at 6:25 P.M., the jumbo jet lifted off from Heathrow and into the air over London.

Right away, Captain MacQuarrie steered the massive aircraft northwest and climbed toward its cruising altitude of 31,000 feet. The airplane's planned route would take it over Lockerbie in southern Scotland and then across the Atlantic Ocean.

Lockerbie is located just north of Scotland's border with England. In the late 1980s, it was a tiny farming village of about 3,500 people.

Down in the tiny village, at 16 Sherwood Crescent,

fourteen-year-old Stephen Flannigan finished eating supper with his family. Then he went to visit his friend David Edwards, who lived half a block away. At 13 Sherwood Crescent, Dora and Maurice Henry prepared to have supper. At their countryside farm three miles away, Jimmie and June Wilson and their daughter, Lesley, relaxed over coffee.

Pan Am 103 soon crossed over the border between England and Scotland. Then, Alan Topp, the air traffic controller at Scotland's Prestwick Airport, began tracking the flight on his radar. The plane appeared on the screen as a small green box with a cross in its center. Topp and Captain MacQuarrie radioed each other:

"Good evening, Scottish," said MacQuarrie to the Scottish air traffic controller. "Clipper One Zero Three. We are level at three one zero."[1] In this manner, MacQuarrie notified Topp that Pan Am 103 had reached its cruising altitude of 31,000 feet.

Topp told MacQuarrie to fly a route that would take him directly over Lockerbie. For a moment, Topp had to monitor another flight. When he looked back at his screen, he noticed that the green box representing Pan Am 103 had disappeared. In its place were four smaller, blinking boxes that seemed to fan out.

Immediately, Topp tried to radio Pan Am 103. "Clipper One Zero Three, Scottish," Topp called.[2] He tried again and again, but MacQuarrie never answered.

Topp's supervisor, Adrian Ford, was already on the radio with a British Airways pilot. The pilot reported that

*T*he impact of Pan Am Flight 103 in Lockerbie left this deep crater in the earth. Twenty homes were destroyed and eleven town residents were killed in the crash.

he had just seen an explosion and gigantic fire on the ground in southern Scotland. Topp felt sick to his stomach as he realized the awful truth. At 7:03 P.M., Pan Am 103 had exploded in midair, nearly six miles above the ground.

Bodies and airplane parts fell from the sky onto Lockerbie. The force of the crash destroyed more than twenty homes in Sherwood Crescent. There, part of the fuselage (the body of the airplane) and its wings, which were filled with jet fuel, exploded when they hit the earth. The impact created a giant crater about half as long as a football field. The force of the explosion killed Maurice and Dora Henry and demolished their house. Stephen Flannigan and David Edwards survived, but Stephen's family perished in the fiery blast. The cockpit of the jumbo jet smashed into the Wilsons' fields, scattering thousands of pieces of debris, such as luggage, airplane parts, and damaged Christmas presents.

Chief Constable John Boyd, head of the area's tiny twenty-two-member police force, quickly organized search parties for possible survivors. He asked for help from neighboring police departments and from the military. Mountain rescue teams, with dogs specially trained to locate survivors, joined in the rescue effort.

However, it was soon clear that all 259 passengers and crew members on board were dead. In addition, eleven residents of Sherwood Crescent perished in the fiery explosion of the jet's wings. The average age of the victims was twenty-seven.

Soon the rescue operation was transformed into a search for what caused the crash. John Boyd and the others investigating the crash suspected that it was not an accident. The 747 aircraft was considered one of the safest in the skies. "We knew in our hearts," Boyd recalled, "that it was not a natural thing that caused the aircraft to break up like that."[3] If the crash of Pan Am 103 was not accidental, then it was the mass murder of 270 innocent victims. The murderers had to be found.

A rescue operation quickly turned into a crime investigation at the crash site of Pan Am Flight 103.

CHAPTER 2

Investigation

Across the Atlantic, many relatives and friends of passengers on Pan Am 103 arrived at JFK Airport, unaware of the disaster. One mother collapsed on the airport floor when she heard the tragic news of her daughter's death. Anguished relatives were inconsolable, saying, "I don't want to live. I don't want to wake up tomorrow."[1] In a private lounge, chaplains offered comfort to the bereaved. Almost immediately, the grief-stricken families, as well as the general public, demanded to know what had caused the disaster. Some relatives took the first available flights and traveled to Lockerbie, hoping to find out more about the tragedy. They were welcomed by the village residents, who were struggling themselves with the effects of the tragedy.

By the morning of December 22, more than 1,100 police officers and 600 military personnel were already on the scene, searching for clues to the cause of the disaster. Officials from both American and British agencies worked together. These agencies included the Federal Aviation Administration (FAA), Federal Bureau of Investigation (FBI), and Central Intelligence Agency (CIA). The Air Accident Investigation Branch (AAIB), a British agency similar to the FAA, joined these American agencies. The village school, Lockerbie Academy, became the command post for the investigation.

From the start, investigators were puzzled at how Pan Am 103 vanished from the air traffic controller's radar screen without any emergency radio call. Also, all of the airplane's communication systems had gone dead at the same time. According to experts, this situation could only have been caused by a midair collision, a complete structural failure, or a bomb-like explosion.

Pan Am 103 did not collide with another jet. Total structural failure was thought to be unlikely. Even though the plane was the fifteenth-oldest 747 in use and had been flying since 1970, most aviation experts did not consider the plane to be especially worn.[2] Aircraft engineers had made many structural repairs and improvements to the plane during an overhaul in 1978. Also, a week before the crash, mechanics had given the aircraft a complete mechanical checkup.

Still, the investigators needed evidence to conclude that a bomb had caused the crash. Finding such evidence would be difficult, since the remains of the aircraft were scattered across an 845-square-mile area surrounding Lockerbie. Wreckage and clothing were found as far as the North Sea, seventy miles away. The body of one woman was recovered, still strapped into her airline seat, more than ten miles from the village.

Chief Constable Boyd stressed the importance of a careful search. "If Flight 103 had left Heathrow on time," he said later, "it would have blown up in the sky over the Atlantic, and there would have been no evidence. Here, we had a chance to get evidence, and it was important to gather as much as we could. We had a chance, and an obligation, to make those people responsible for this tragedy pay for it."[3]

Searchers put each item they found into a separate clear plastic bag and brought the bags to the command center. An X-ray machine tested every piece of luggage, clothing, and other debris for traces of explosives.

A bomb large enough to destroy a 747 would leave telltale signs. The force of the explosion would send pieces of the bomb and anything near it bursting outward. These fragments would embed themselves into whatever they contacted, such as nearby luggage or the skin of the aircraft, and leave a certain type of small dent. Walter Korsgaard, an FAA expert on aircraft explosions, called these damaging marks "unique," and added, "You don't find them in any other kind of impact."[4] Korsgaard showed investigators many photographs of this type of damage so that they would know what to look for.

On Christmas Day, searchers located a piece of metal that looked just like one of Walter Korsgaard's photographs. Later other pieces were found. They proved conclusively that a bomb had brought down Pan Am 103.

Investigators also found pieces of a radio-cassette player that had been fitted with Semtex, a plastic explosive. Semtex can be molded like clay to fit into small spaces. It is nearly impossible to detect, since it does not look like a bomb. The player had been hidden in a suitcase, which was loaded into the forward cargo bay. When it exploded, it blew a giant hole in the side of the aircraft and destroyed the plane's entire electrical system.

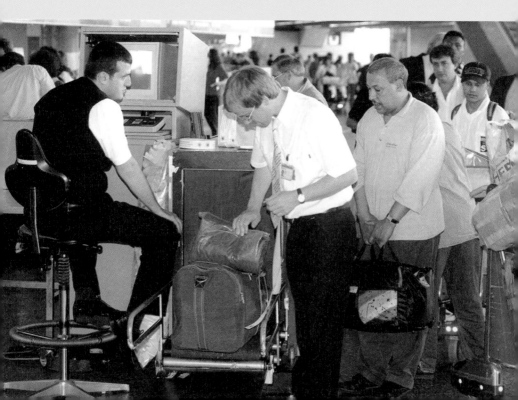

X-ray security measures like those in this airport in Frankfurt, Germany, have increased since the Pan Am Flight 103 explosion in 1988.

Since the bomb was specifically designed to blow up an airplane in midair, detectives suspected that terrorists had placed it aboard Pan Am 103. Terrorists use threats and violence to try to force a government to make political and social changes. They may blow up buildings or airplanes or hijack aircraft, demanding that the pilot fly to a certain location. Terrorists believe that governments will give in to their demands in order to avoid future violence.

One terrorist group that came under immediate suspicion was the Popular Front for the Liberation of Palestine—General Command (PFLP-GC), founded by Ahmed Jibril. The PFLP-GC had often committed terrorism against Israel and its supporters, such as the United States. In October 1988, Frankfurt police had arrested members of the PFLP-GC for possessing a bomb similar to the one that destroyed Pan Am 103. Three weeks after the arrest, the Federal Aviation Administration (FAA) sent a security alert to all U.S. airlines describing the cassette-recorder bomb. The warning cautioned that such bombs were almost impossible to detect. However, the bulletin never arrived at Pan Am's baggage operations in Frankfurt.

A few weeks before the crash, a specific bomb threat had been made against Pan Am. On December 5, 1988, an anonymous caller with a thick Arabic accent telephoned the U.S. Embassy in Helsinki, Finland. He said that before the end of the year, members of an Arab terrorist organization would smuggle a bomb on board a Pan Am flight from Frankfurt to the United States. The American embassy notified Pan Am, but neither the airline nor

*A*hmed Jibril (left), founder of the PFLP-GC, is shown here seated next to Abu Moussa, leader of the Fatah-Uprising—a separate group also dedicated to the liberation of Palestine.

Finnish officials took the call seriously. Still, the FAA issued a warning on December 7, 1988, to all airlines and airports in Europe, advising them to increase security. Although the U.S. Department of State forwarded the FAA bulletin to all of its European embassies, the only embassy that posted the warning was in Moscow.

Passengers on Pan Am 103 were unaware of what became known as the Helsinki warning. After the crash, many relatives of the victims expressed outrage that neither the airline nor the U.S. government had notified the public of the threat. Government agencies countered that they receive many such threats, most of which prove to be false.[5]

At 5:00 A.M. on December 22, a telephone call seemed to provide specific evidence that terrorists were responsible for the crash. In London, a man called the offices of two important news reporting services, the Associated Press and the United Press International. He claimed to represent the Guardians of the Islamic Revolution. He

Mourners are shown carrying coffins through the streets of Tehran, Iran, on July 7, 1988, just days after the U.S.S. *Vincennes* shot down an Iranian passenger jet.

said that his group had blown up Pan Am 103 as revenge for the U.S.S. *Vincennes*'s accidental shooting down of Iran Air Flight 655 the previous July. The *Vincennes* had mistakenly identified the regularly-scheduled commercial jet as an Iranian F-14 fighter plane. The U.S. warship was patrolling the Persian Gulf, guarding oil tankers from possible attack. When radio operators on the Vincennes tried to contact the Iranian plane, the civilian pilot never received the messages because they were sent over a radio frequency that only military aircraft use. After Iran Air 655 failed to answer any of the ship's radio commands, the officers on the *Vincennes* assumed it was an enemy plane and shot it down. All 340 on board, including sixty-three children, died. The captain of the *Vincennes* apologized and the United States called the incident an unfortunate accident taking place in a war zone. However, Iran considered it an unprovoked act of war.

In the past, terrorist groups connected with Iran had sought revenge in such situations. However, intelligence experts knew of no organization called the Guardians of the Islamic Revolution. Clearly, investigators needed more information before they could determine which terrorist group, if any, was responsible for the crash of Pan Am 103.

CHAPTER 3

Security
Concerns

At the time of the Pan Am 103 crash, the FAA had already established strict rules about checking in passengers and handling baggage in order to decrease the risk of terrorist attacks. However, the FAA did not consistently enforce these rules, nor did Pan Am always follow them. Pan Am was especially lax in handling interline baggage (luggage transferred from one airline to another).

FAA rules stated that if a checked bag could not be matched to someone who was on board a flight, then that bag had to be opened and searched. Also, any baggage that belonged to a person who did not appear for a flight had to be removed from the flight and searched. These actions were designed to prevent a terrorist from hiding a bomb in unaccompanied luggage or tricking an unsuspecting passenger into bringing a bomb on board.

Several months prior to the Pan Am 103 disaster, the airline's officials stopped searching unaccompanied bags.

They also stopped matching bags to passengers. These actions were in direct violation of FAA regulations.

Other security problems may have led to the bomb being smuggled on board Pan Am 103. Ulrich Weber, Pan Am's chief of security at Frankfurt Airport, lacked specialized training. He also hired several unqualified security workers. Further, Pan Am employees working at the Frankfurt Airport had not been told about the State Department's Helsinki warning. They also never received the November 1988 FAA warning about radio-cassette bombs. As a result, Pan Am baggage inspectors were not on the alert for suspicious-looking cassette recorders.

Within weeks after the disaster, relatives of the victims met to provide support for each other. They wanted to work with government officials to find out why the explosion had occurred and to look for ways to prevent future terrorist attacks. On February 19, 1989, they formed a group called Victims of Pan Am Flight 103. A similar group, the United Kingdom Families of Flight 103, was formed in Great Britain.

Within six months, leaders of the Victims of Pan Am Flight 103 disagreed about the organization's goals and leadership styles. Some of the members formed a new group, Families of Pan Am Flight 103, Lockerbie. The meetings of this group focused more specifically on improving airline security.

Leaders from the two American groups lobbied government officials for an independent investigation into the cause of the tragedy. As a result, then-President

J ack Flynn pauses to compose himself while discussing the experience of losing his son, John Patrick Flynn, on Pan Am Flight 103 during a conference that took place in April 2001.

George Bush appointed a seven-member commission. Its job was to identify ways to prevent future terrorist attacks. In May 1990, the President's Commission on Aviation Security and Terrorism published its 182-page report, which strongly criticized the FAA, the State Department, and the aviation industry.[1] It placed much of the blame for the disaster on a "seriously flawed" aviation security system and noted, "The destruction of Flight 103 may well have been preventable."[2] The commission found that Pan Am was guilty of "apparent security lapses" that remained uncorrected nine months after the bombing.[3] Although at that time investigators did not know for sure how the bomb had gotten on the flight, they concluded

*V*ice President Al Gore headed the Gore Commission that recommended improvements in explosives detection in luggage.

from the passenger list that no terrorist had been on board. It was clear that major security problems existed with the screening of luggage and passengers.

As a result of the bombing of Pan Am 103, public concern spread about airline safety. Congress responded by adopting the Aviation Security Improvement Act of 1990. This law required the FAA to develop standards for equipment that would detect explosives in luggage.

Within months of the disaster, the FAA fined Pan Am $630,000 for violating security rules at Frankfurt and Heathrow airports. Pan Am hired a new security firm and security director, but it was too late to save the airline's reputation. Customers were afraid to fly on Pan Am. During the year after the crash, the airline lost $306 million. Pan Am, which had been experiencing financial problems for many years, ceased operations on December 4, 1991.

In August 1996, President Bill Clinton ordered a special commission to review all aviation safety issues. Titled the White House Commission on Aviation Safety and

Security, it was known as the Gore Commission, since Vice President Al Gore was in charge of it. In February 1997, the Gore Commission recommended improvements in explosives detection in luggage. This included the use of new machines that could literally peer into luggage and detect small amounts of explosives.[4] The commission also urged the use of machines which could detect extremely small amounts of explosives. Some of these machines are walk-through devices that scan passengers' clothing, while others check for traces of explosives on tickets or boarding passes.[5] One of the newest screening machines uses pencil-thin X-ray beams to scan luggage for any traces of explosives. Today, U.S. airports have to screen all checked bags for explosives.[6] Airlines are now required to make sure that no passenger's bags are flown on a flight unless the passenger is also on the flight.

The loss of Pan Am 103 was a terrible disaster. While improvements have since been made in airline security, the lives of victims' families would never be the same.

CHAPTER 4

Aftermath

Relatives of the Pan Am 103 victims reacted to the tragedy in a variety of ways. Some have gone through years of grief counseling. Others have raised money to fund scholarships dedicated to the memories of those they lost in the tragedy. Some have formed friendships from the family support groups that were founded after the disaster. In 1995, two new family groups developed: Justice for Pan Am 103 and Terrorism Watch: Pan Am 103. These groups also oppose terrorism and work to improve airline security. Sometimes they have different opinions on how to achieve these goals.

Some of the bereaved have become outspoken advocates for airline safety. Victoria Cummock, whose husband, John, died in the bombing, became an active member of the Families of Pan Am 103, Lockerbie. She has testified before Congress and was a member of the White House Commission on Aviation Safety and Security.

*D*aniel and Susan Cohen hold a picture of their daughter, Theodora, a Syracuse University student who lost her life in the Pan Am Flight 103 explosion.

Daniel and Susan Cohen are tireless activists against terrorism. Their daughter, Theo, was one of the Syracuse University students who perished in the crash. They have written *Pan Am 103*, a book which describes their grief and anger over the tragedy and their search for justice for their daughter's murder.

Geri Buser lost her husband, son, and pregnant daughter in the tragedy. She, like many of the victims' relatives, finds comfort in frequent visits to Lockerbie, where she has formed a friendship with Ella Ramsden. The bodies of Buser's husband and daughter were found in the wreckage of Ramsden's home.

Others share Buser's affection for the villagers, who gathered up the blood-stained clothing of the victims, washed and ironed it, and mailed it back to their relatives, carefully wrapped in tissue paper. "We were told by the State Department that we couldn't have the clothes back," said Aphrodite Tsairis, whose nineteen-year-old daughter, Alexia, died in the crash. "They said that things were too badly damaged. But the people of Lockerbie just did it. I can't tell you what that meant to us."[1]

Georgia Nucci lost her son, Chris, in the explosion. Tragically, her daughter, Jennifer, died of a tropical disease the year before while an exchange student in Ecuador. "For about a month after each child died, it was as if I had had major surgery," Nucci recalled. "That kind of grief is very physical."[2] Nucci remembered what Chris had told her when Jennifer died: "Don't get all weepy. . . . That makes a negative out of her whole life."[3] Nucci decided to help the other families of victims recall the good memories they had of their loved ones. She assembled a book of family stories and photos remembering the victims.

Still, this activity was not enough to fill the loss Nucci felt. "As a consequence of terrorism, I was no longer a mother," she said.[4] She and her husband, Tony, visited an orphanage in Bogota, Colombia, in August 1990. There, they adopted four children, ages four through twelve.

Artist Suse Lowenstein expressed her grief in sculpture. First she created a sculpture representing the moment she learned of the death of her son, Alexander.[5] Then she asked other women whose family members had died on the flight to come to her studio. She photographed them in the position that each of them had taken when they realized their loss. She created a sculpture from these images and titled it *Dark Elegy*. Within each sculpture is a personal memento of that victim. The sculpture "is a large part of my coping and dealing with Alexander's death," Lowenstein said. "Healing is the wrong word because the wound of losing Alexander will never heal. But the project gives me comfort."[6]

In 1998, on the tenth anniversary of the Pan Am 103 disaster, ceremonies were held to remember the victims. Services in Great Britain and the United States began at 7:03 P.M. (2:03 P.M. ET in the U.S.), the same moment the bomb went off on December 21, 1988. In Lockerbie, Prince Philip, husband of Britain's Queen Elizabeth II, laid a wreath in the Garden of Remembrance in Dryfesdale

*S*amples of sculpture from Suse Lowenstein's *Dark Elegy*. Lowenstein lost her son, Alexander, in the Pan Am 103 bombing.

Cemetery. There, a simple polished stone memorial lists the names of the 270 victims. Some of the relatives of American victims attended the ceremony in Lockerbie. Bert Ammerman, brother of victim Thomas Ammerman, said, "My family's expanded at the expense of the death of my brother. These people, the people of Pan Am 103, have become my family."[7]

President Bill Clinton attended a ceremony at Arlington National Cemetery, where the official U.S. memorial is located. The memorial is a cairn (a cone-shaped stack of stones). The stones that make up the cairn

*A*ttorney General Janet Reno, National Security Adviser Anthony Lake and Secretary of State Warren Christopher (from left to right) attend a memorial service for the Pan Am victims in November 1995.

were taken from a Lockerbie quarry. In all, there are 270 stones in the cairn. Each stone represents a victim of the bombing.

At the beginning of the Arlington service, the names of each of the victims was read aloud by a family member. President Clinton spoke directly to the families of the victims: "Although ten years, or twenty or thirty or fifty, may never be long enough for the sorrow to fade, we pray that it may not be too long now before the wait for justice and resolution is over."[8]

President Clinton's words were prophetic. Two suspects in the bombing would soon go on trial.

The memorial cairn erected for the Pan Am 103 victims that stands in the Arlington National Cemetery.

CHAPTER 5

Finally, the Trial

After years of suspicions pointing to Iran and Syria as being responsible for the Pan Am 103 disaster, U.S. and British authorities located new evidence. It pointed to the North African nation of Libya, where many terrorist groups have ties. Investigators located thumbnail-sized fragments of the bomb's timing device, which they traced to a Swiss company, MEBO AG. MEBO had sold the timer to a high-level official in the JSO, Libya's intelligence service.

Clothing packed in the suitcase that held the bomb contained traces of Semtex. One of the items of clothing bore a label from the Malta Trading Company. The clothing was traced to Mary's House, a store on the Mediterranean island of Malta. Tony Gauci, the store owner, remembered selling the clothing to an Arabic man just before Christmas in 1988. He recalled that the man's accent seemed to be Libyan.

Investigators found that the suitcase containing the

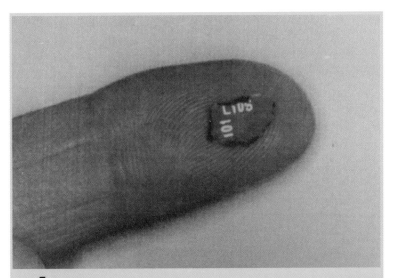

*I*nvestigators found fragments of a bomb's timing device in the Pan Am wreckage that were smaller than a thumbnail. These fragments helped put investigators on the trail of the bombing suspects.

bomb could have been transferred at Frankfurt from a flight that came from Malta. Al-Amin Khalifah Fhimah, an employee of Libyan Arab Airlines on Malta, and Abdel Baset al-Megrahi, a JSO agent, immediately came under suspicion.

In 1991, the United States and Great Britain filed murder charges against al-Megrahi and Fhimah. They demanded that Libya turn the two suspects over for trial. However, Libyan leader Moammar Khadafy refused to surrender the suspects, claiming that they would not receive a fair trial. On January 21, 1992, the United Nations Security Council insisted that Libya hand over the suspects. When Khadafy ignored these demands, the Security

Council imposed sanctions, or restrictions, on air travel and arms sales to Libya. In this manner, the U.N. hoped to apply economic pressure to force Libya to release the suspects. The United States imposed sanctions of its own and, in March 1995, offered a $4-million reward for the capture of the suspects.

In the meantime, diplomats worked to arrange a compromise regarding a location for the trial. In July 1998, U.S. and British authorities agreed that the trial could be held in a neutral location. On April 5, 1999, the two Libyan suspects surrendered to U.N. authorities for trial.

With the two suspects in the bombing in custody, the U.N. suspended its sanctions against Libya. But the United States has continued its restrictions on business dealings with Libya. Government officials are waiting for Libya to admit responsibility for the attack. Libya must also pay the victims' families compensation, or money paid as punishment, for its suspected involvement in the disaster, before any of the U.S. restrictions will be eased.

The trial began on May 3, 2000, in the Netherlands near the city of Utrecht at Camp Zeist, a former U.S. military base. It was considered Scottish soil for purposes of the trial. The trial was held before three Scottish judges and under Scottish law, since the explosion had occurred over Scotland.

The prosecutors charged that al-Megrahi and Fhimah hid the radio-cassette bomb in a brown hard-sided Samsonite suitcase. Together, they allegedly smuggled the suitcase on board an Air Malta flight at Malta's Luqa

*I*n November 1991, Assistant Attorney General Robert Mueller III (above) announced the indictment of two citizens of Libya for the bombing of Pan Am Flight 103.

Airport. From there, the suitcase went to Frankfurt, where it was transferred to the flight connecting to Pan Am 103. Throughout its journey, the suitcase remained undetected as unaccompanied baggage. In his testimony, Tony Gauci identified a photograph of al-Megrahi as the purchaser of the clothing from his store. He also noted in a police identification lineup and in court that the suspect closely resembled the purchaser.[1]

The defense lawyers maintained that the suspects were innocent. They said that two Palestinian terrorist groups based in Syria were responsible for the tragedy. These groups were the Popular Front for the Liberation

GIVE US THESE TERRORISTS. WE'LL GIVE YOU UP TO $4 MILLION.

Wanted posters printed in English and Arabic offered a $4-million reward for bombing suspects Abdel Baset al-Megrahi and Al-Amin Khalifa Fhimah.

of Palestine-General Command (PFLP-GC) and the Palestinian Popular Struggle Front (PPSF).

On January 31, 2001, the three Scottish judges found al-Megrahi guilty of murder. Fhimah was found not guilty and released. Al-Megrahi appealed his conviction—filing legal papers that requested a new trial. On March 14, 2002, this appeal was denied. Al-Megrahi began serving a life sentence in Scotland's Barlinnie Prison immediately. He must serve at least twenty years of this sentence before he can be considered for parole.

When they announced their verdict against al-Megrahi, the judges noted that there were "a number of uncertainties and qualifications."[2] Prosecutors were not able to prove conclusively how the suitcase was loaded onto the flight in Malta. They were only able to show that one of the suspects, al-Megrahi, was a high-ranking member of the JSO. The case against Fhimah was dismissed because it relied mainly on the testimony of Abdul Majid Giaka, a former Libyan spy and CIA agent, who gave contradictory evidence. No evidence proved that any other terrorist groups were involved with the bombing. Still, the judges felt the evidence against al-Megrahi came together "to form a real and convincing pattern."[3]

Many relatives of the Pan Am 103 victims had flown to Camp Zeist to be there when the verdicts were announced. They hugged each other and cried when they heard the verdicts. Bert Ammerman commented that the families "got some justice today."[4]

Many of the relatives believe that the verdict against

al-Megrahi points to Libya's leader, Moammar Khadafy, as being responsible for this terrorist bombing. Bryan Flynn, whose brother, John Patrick Flynn, died in the disaster, said: "It's a guilty verdict against the Libyan government. We believe Moammar Khadafy ordered it. He should be tried as a war criminal."[5] Still, some victims' families expressed disappointment in the sentence since it amounted to less than one month for each victim of the disaster.[6]

Many of the relatives promised to push for action on their civil suit filed in federal court in New York City. They are suing the Libyan government to obtain money as punishment for its alleged involvement in the disaster. The conviction of al-Megrahi supplies a link to the Libyan government, which strengthens the relatives' case.

Libya is now under both economic and political pressure to settle the case. Experts estimate that the U.N. sanctions alone cost Libya between $20 and $30 billion.[7] The Libyan government is interested in re-obtaining U.S. investments in agriculture and oil. These investments will not resume until the case is settled. Recently, Libya itself has been attacked by terrorists. The Islamic Fighting Group, or IFG, has repeatedly tried to overthrow Moammar Khadafy's government. As a result of these attacks, Khadafy seems interested in joining other nations, such as the United States, who are fighting against terrorism.[8] Thus, Khadafy now appears willing to consider accepting at least some responsibility for the Pan Am bombing.

*A*bdel Baset al-Megrahi was convicted of murder by three Scottish judges on January 31, 2001.

Both the British and U.S. governments have been working together to pressure Libya to pay compensation to the victims' families. In October 2001, they moved a step closer to achieving this goal. They met with Musa Kusa, a Libyan intelligence leader suspected of planning many terrorist acts, including the bombing of Pan Am 103. Officials at these meetings said that Kusa appeared to be laying the foundation for the settlement of the Pan Am case.[9] The government of Libya was expected to offer a financial settlement and most likely would accept responsibility for the Pan Am bombing. However, Moammar Khadafy and other Libyan officials probably would not admit prior knowledge of the attack.[10]

To show that his government was trying to cooperate with British and American officials, Kusa identified suspected members of Al Qaeda, the terrorist network headed by Osama bin Laden. Bin Laden, whose family lives in Saudi Arabia, operated out of Afghanistan. From there, he

*L*ibyan leader Moammar Khadafy is shown here at a press conference on February 5, 2001, stating that he can prove Libya was not involved in the bombing of Pan Am Flight 103.

allegedly planned the largest terrorist act ever committed against the United States. On September 11, 2001, nineteen Arab terrorists killed themselves as well as about 3,000 innocent victims when they hijacked and destroyed four U.S. commercial airliners. The hijackers used the airliners as flying bombs. Two aircraft crashed into the Twin

A great fireball erupts as a hijacked 767 passenger jet collides with one of the Twin Towers of the World Trade Center in New York City on the morning of September 11, 2001.

Towers of the World Trade Center in New York City, killing all on board the aircraft as well as thousands in the buildings. Another nosedived into the Pentagon, the headquarters of the U.S. Department of Defense in Washington, D.C. A fourth airliner crashed into a field near Pittsburgh, Pennsylvania. Officials suspect that passengers on that plane overpowered the hijackers, preventing them from crashing the aircraft into their planned target. This target was most likely an important government building, such as the White House.

The tragic events of September 11, 2001, brought back memories of the crash of Pan Am 103 to the victims' families. Marjorie McQueen, a government official in Lockerbie, called the size of the terrorist attack against the United States "just unbelievable."[11] McQueen's children, who were on vacation in New York City on September 11, had planned to visit the World Trade Center that day. For a time, McQueen feared that her son and daughter had been killed in the terrorist attacks. Although she soon learned that her relatives were safe, McQueen said that she could not stop shaking. She added, "We had a lot of support from the American side after the Lockerbie disaster. Now our thoughts are with them."[12] Hours after the September 11 disaster, Pamela Dix, whose brother, Peter Dix, was killed in the Pan Am 103 bombing, said: "It's times like this that those of us who have experienced something of this nature are drawn together."[13]

Other Terrorist Acts

DATE	EVENT
September 5, 1972	Arab terrorists shoot and kill eleven members of the Israeli Olympic team at the Summer Olympic Games in Munich, Germany.
November 4, 1979	Iranian revolutionaries storm the U.S. Embassy in Tehran, Iran, and hold fifty-two Americans hostage for 444 days before finally releasing them on January 21, 1981.
October 23, 1983	Shiite Muslim suicide bomber drives a truck full of explosives into an airport building full of sleeping U.S. Marines in Beirut, Lebanon, resulting in 241 deaths.
October 7, 1985	The Italian cruise ship *Achille Lauro* is hijacked by four members of the Palestine Liberation Organization (PLO) near Port Said, Egypt. One male American passenger is shot and thrown overboard before the hijackers surrender.
September 19, 1989	Libyan terrorists bomb UTA Flight 772 over Niger, killing 171.
April 10, 1992	The Irish Republican Army (IRA) sets off a car bomb in London, England. Three people are killed and ninety-one others are injured.
February 26, 1993	A car bomb explodes in the basement garage of the World Trade Center in New York, killing six and injuring more than a thousand others.
March 20, 1995	Japanese terrorists release sarin gas in five Tokyo subway cars, killing twelve and injuring about 5,500 others.
April 19, 1995	Federal Building in Oklahoma City is bombed in a plot led by American right-wing extremist Timothy McVeigh. One hundred sixty-eight people are killed; hundreds of others injured.
February 25, 1996	The Palestinian terrorist group Hamas bombs an Israeli bus in West Jerusalem. Twenty-four passengers and the bomber are killed.
April 18, 1996	Islamic militants shoot and kill eighteen Greek tourists outside a hotel in Cairo, Egypt.
August 7, 1998	U.S. embassies in Kenya and Tanzania, Africa, are bombed by al Qaeda terrorists almost simultaneously, killing 263 and injuring about 5,000 others.
October 12, 2000	Motorboats loaded with explosives are driven by al Qaeda terrorists into the U.S.S. *Cole* in the Yemeni port of Aden, killing seventeen American sailors.
September 11, 2001	Four commercial jets are hijacked; two crash into the Twin Towers of the World Trade Center in New York, ultimately causing the buildings to collapse, killing thousands; the third jet crashes into the Pentagon just outside Washington, D.C.; the fourth crashes in western Pennsylvania.

Chapter Notes

Chapter 1: December 21, 1988
1. Steven Emerson and Brian Duffy, *The Fall of Pan Am 103: Inside the Lockerbie Investigation* (New York: Penguin Putnam, Inc., 1990), p. 17.
2. Ibid., p. 18.
3. Ibid., p. 31.

Chapter 2: Investigation
1. Matthew Cox and Tom Foster, *Their Darkest Day: The Tragedy of Pan Am 103 and Its Legacy of Hope* (New York: Grove Weidenfeld, 1992), p. 77.
2. William E. Smith, "Terror in the Night," *Time*, January 2, 1989, p. 75.
3. Emerson and Duffy, p. 38.
4. Ibid., p. 85.
5. Smith, p. 75.

Chapter 3: Security Concerns
1. Matthew Cox and Tom Foster, *Their Darkest Day: The Tragedy of Pan Am 103 and Its Legacy of Hope* (New York: Grove Weidenfeld, 1992), p. 161.
2. Don Phillips and George Lardner Jr., "Laxity by Pan Am, FAA Blamed in Jet Bombing," *The Washington Post*, May 16, 1990, p. A1.
3. Cox and Foster, p. 161.
4. U.S. Department of Transportation, White House Commission on Aviation and Security: The DOT Status Report (Washington, D.C.: U.S. Department of Transportation, February 1998).
5. Ibid.
6. Jim Erickson, "DIA May Test New Bag X-ray," *The Rocky Mountain News*, December 20, 2001, page 4A.

Chapter 4: Aftermath
1. George Rosie, "Left Behind by Lockerbie," *Independent on Sunday*, December 6, 1998, p. 6.
2. Michael Ryan, "The World is Full of Children to Love," *Parade*, July 15, 2001, p. 4.
3. Ibid., p. 5.
4. Ibid.
5. Joan Deppa, with Maria Russell, Dona Hayes and Elizabeth Lynne Flocke, *The Media and Disasters: Pan Am 103* (New York: New York University Press, 1994), p. 62.

6. Rosie, p. 6.

7. "Tenth Anniversary of Lockerbie Bomb Observed," *CNN.com*, December 21, 1998, <http://www.cnn.com/US/9812/21/lockerbie.memorials/> (February 1, 2002).

8. "Calls for Justice Come on Tenth Anniversary of Lockerbie Bombing," *CNN.com*, December 21, 1998, <http://www.cnn.com/US/9812/21/lockerbie.memorial.02/> (February 1, 2002).

Chapter 5: Finally, the Trial

1. Lord Sutherland, *In the High Court of Justiciary at Camp Zeist*, Case No: 1475/99, Opinion of the Court, p. 66.

2. Ibid., p. 81.

3. Ibid., p. 82.

4. "Relatives Focus Anger on Libya," *CNN.com*, January 31, 2001, <http://www.cnn.com/2001/WORLD/europe/01/31/lockerbie.family.03/index.html> (February 1, 2002).

5. Peter Finn, "One Guilty, One Free in Pan Am Bombing," *The Denver Post*, February 1, 2001, p. 5A.

6. Ibid., pp. 1A and 5A.

7. "Interview with *Price of Terror* co-author Allan Gerson," *CNN.Com Community*, November 14, 2001, <http://www.cnn.com/2001/COMMUNITY/11/14/gerson/index.html> (January 29, 2002).

8. Ibid.

9. John Walcott, "U.S. Officials Secretly Met Terror Suspect," *Fort Worth Star Telegram*, October 21, 2001, <http://www.geocities.com/CapitolHill/5260/knightridder211001.html> (January 29, 2002).

10. Marc Perelman, "Bush Administration's Orchestrating a Thaw with Gadhafi's [sic] Libya," *The Forward*, October 19, 2001, <http://www.geocities.com/CapitolHill/5260/forward191001.html> (January 29, 2002).

11. Deirdre Kelly, "Lockerbie Memories Flood Back," *BBC News Online*, September 12, 2001, <http://www.news.bbc.co.uk/hi/english/uk/scotland/newsid_1539000/1539525.stm> (January 29, 2002).

12. Ibid.

13. Ibid.

air traffic controller—A person who directs and monitors different aircraft and keeps track of their progress by radar and radio.

altitude—The height of an object above the earth's surface.

cairn—A stack of stones erected as a memorial or landmark.

debris—The remains of something that has been destroyed.

fuselage—The body of an aircraft. It is the exterior and interior central portions of an airplane which house the crew, passengers, and cargo.

hijack—To seize control of an airplane.

intelligence service—The secret service or organization of a government responsible for spying and gathering secret information about other nations.

interline baggage—Luggage transferred from one airline to another.

plastic explosive—A type of material used to make bombs. It is difficult to detect because it can be molded to fit inside devices such as radios or formed into thin sheets to hide in luggage.

radar—A device used to find aircraft by reflecting radio waves off of them. Radar screens are used to track the progress of airplanes.

sanctions—Restrictions placed by one government or organization on another to apply economic pressure.

structural failure—The destruction of an aircraft that occurs when the fuselage and its mechanical systems totally cease functioning.

terrorist—Someone who seeks to achieve political goals by spreading fear, usually through the threat or act of violence.

verdict—The judgement or decision in a trial.

Further Reading

Cohen, Susan and Daniel. *Pan Am 103.* New York: New American Library, 2000.

Fridell, Ron. *Terrorism: Political Violence at Home and Abroad.* Berkeley Heights, N.J.: Enslow Publishers, Inc., 2001.

Gaffney, Thomas K. *Air Safety: Preventing Future Disasters.* Berkeley Heights, N.J.: Enslow Publishers, Inc., 1999.

Gaines, Ann Graham. *Terrorism.* Philadelphia, Pa.: Chelsea House, 1999.

Gow, Mary. *Attack on America: The Day the Twin Towers Collapsed.* Berkeley Heights, N.J.: Enslow Publishers, Inc., 2002.

Horton, Madelyn. *The Lockerbie Airline Crash.* San Diego, Calif.: Lucent Books, Inc., 1991.

Landau, Elaine. *Air Crashes.* New York: Franklin Watts, 1999.

Internet Addresses

Victims of Pan Am Flight 103
http://web.syr.edu/~vpaf103/index.html

Remembering Lockerbie
http://www.law.syr.edu/academics/academics.asp?what=lockerbie

CNN In-Depth Specials: Reports on the Lockerbie Trial
http://www.cnn.com/LAW/trials.and.cases/case.files/0010/lockerbie/sites.html